MUSE

DRONES

Art Direction & illustrations by Matt Mahurin

Music arranged by Olly Weeks

© 2015 by Faber Music Limited. First published by Faber Music Limited in 2015. Bloomsbury House, 74-77 Great Russell Street, London WC1B 3DA.

ISBN 978-1-4950-4531-8

HAL•LEONARD®
CORPORATION
7777 W. Bluemound Rd. P.O. Box 13819 Milwaukee, WI 53213

In Australia Contact:
Hal Leonard Australia Pty. Ltd.
4 Lentara Court
Cheltenham, Victoria, 3192 Australia
Email: ausadmin@halleonard.com.au

Visit Hal Leonard Online at
www.halleonard.com

TO ME 'DRONES' ARE METAPHORICAL PSYCHOPATHS
WHICH ENABLE PSYCHOPATHIC BEHAVIOUR
WITH NO RECOURSE. THE WORLD IS RUN
BY DRONES UTILIZING DRONES TO TURN US
ALL INTO DRONES. 'DRONES' EXPLORES THE JOURNEY
OF A HUMAN, FROM THEIR ABANDONMENT AND LOSS
OF HOPE, TO THEIR INDOCTRINATION BY THE
SYSTEM TO BE A HUMAN DRONE, TO THEIR
EVENTUAL DEFECTION FROM THEIR OPPRESSORS.

'DEAD INSIDE' IS WHERE THE STORY OF THE ALBUM
BEGINS, WHERE THE PROTAGONIST LOSES HOPE AND
BECOMES 'DEAD INSIDE', THEREFORE VULNERABLE TO
THE DARK FORCES INTRODUCED IN 'PSYCHO' AND WHICH
ENSUE OVER THE NEXT FEW SONGS ON THE ALBUM, BEFORE
EVENTUALLY DEFECTING, REVOLTING AND OVERCOMING
THESE DARK FORCES LATER IN THE STORY.

MATT BELLAMY ON 'DRONES'

Dead Inside

Words and Music by Matthew Bellamy

(Dead in - side.)

1. Re - vere_____ a mil - lion prayers_____ and draw
2. You're free_____ to touch the sky_____ whilst I

_____ me in - to your ho - li - ness.   But there's noth - ing there,
_____ am crushed and_ pul - ver - ised,   be - cause you need con - trol,___

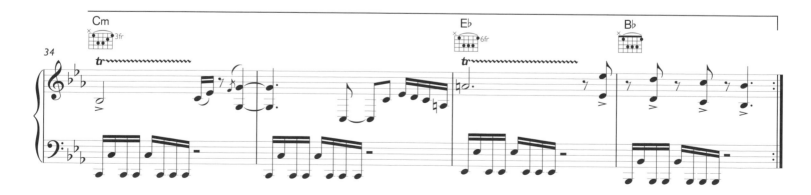

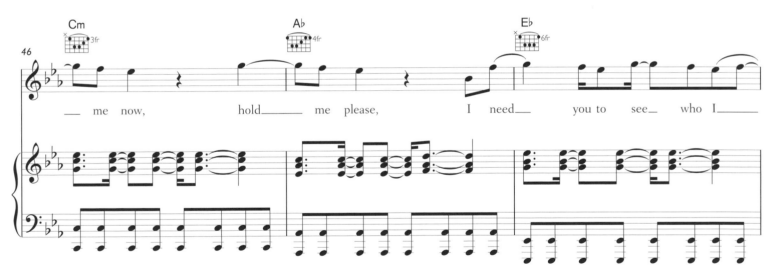

__ me now, hold_____ me please, I need__ you to see_ who I_____

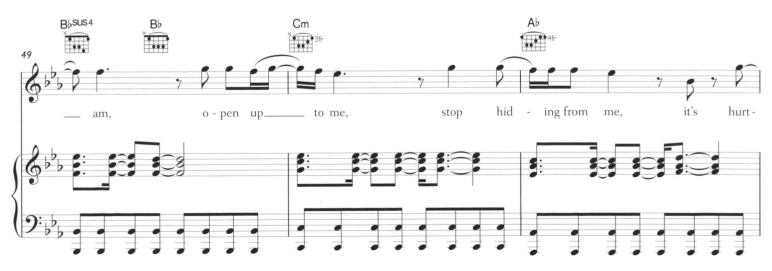

__ am, o-pen up____ to me, stop hid - ing from me, it's hurt-

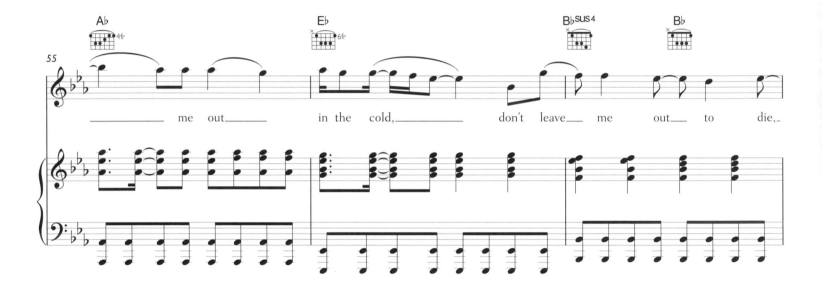

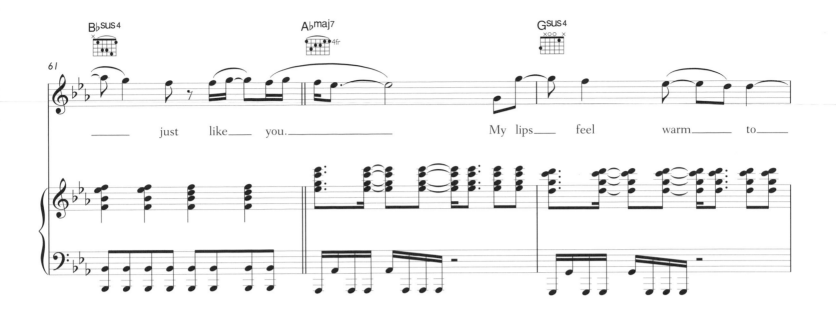

just like___ you.___ My lips___ feel warm___ to___

___ the touch,___ my words___ seem so a - live,___ my skin

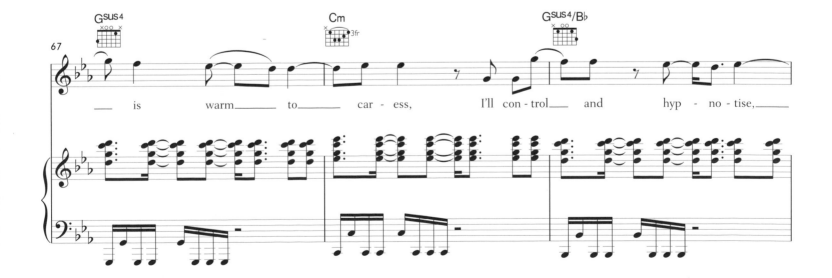

___ is warm___ to___ car - ess, I'll con - trol___ and hyp - no - tise,___

12

PSYCHO

Words and Music by Matthew Bellamy

Tune Guitar:
6 = D (lowest string)
Drop D Tuning

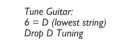

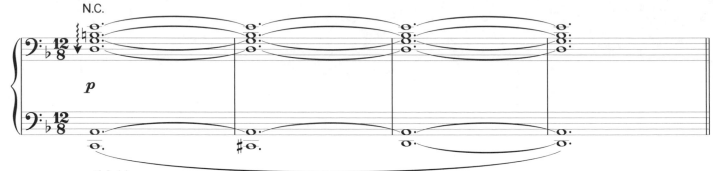

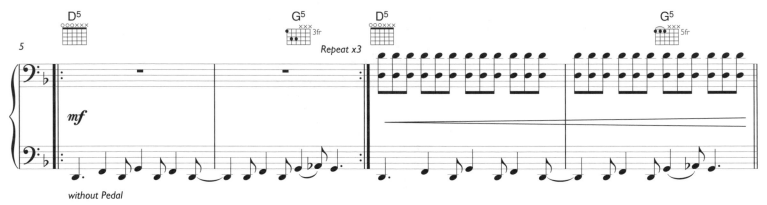

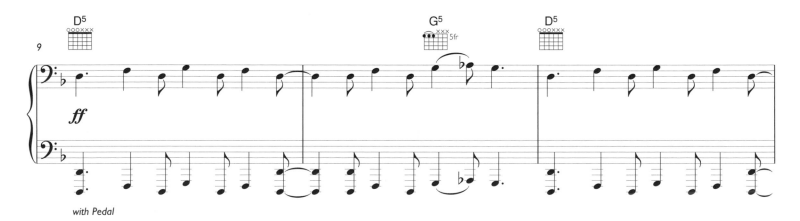

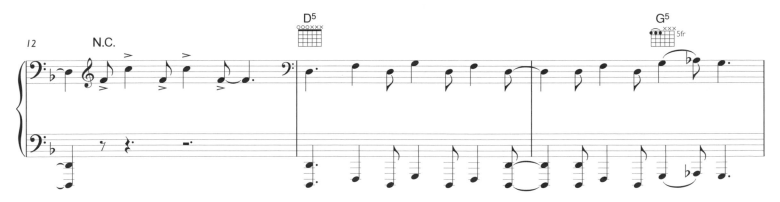

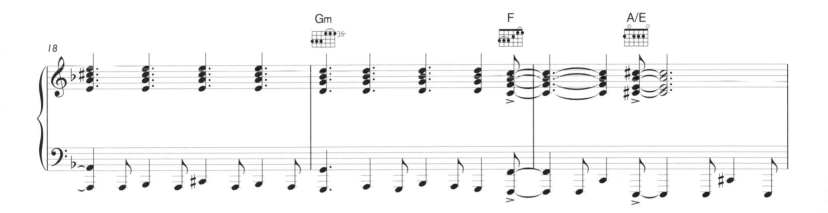

1. Love,   it will get you   no - - where,

(2.) mind   is   just a   pro - - gram

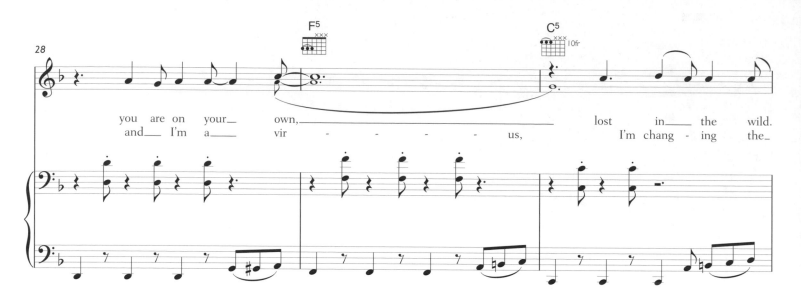

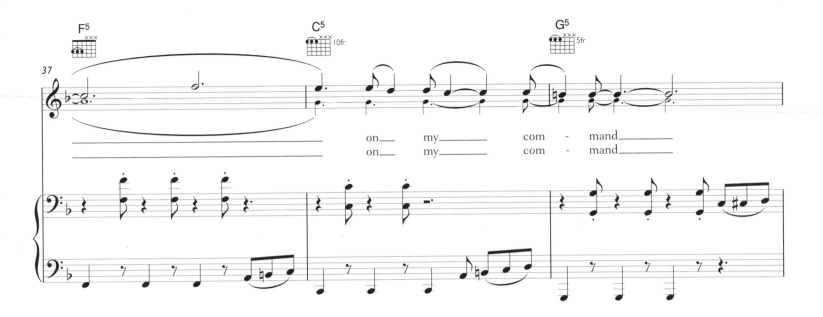

a fuck - ing psy - cho,__

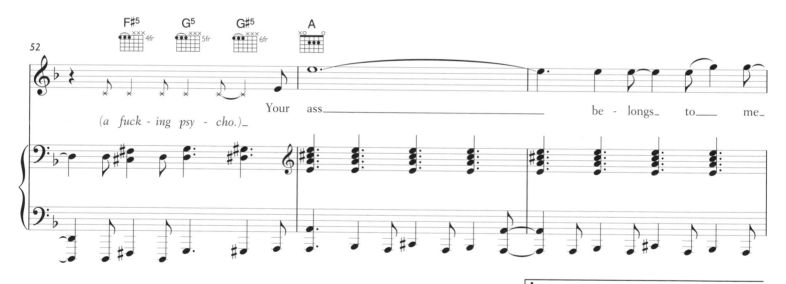

(a fuck - ing psy - cho.)__

Your ass_____ be - longs__ to__ me__

__ now,_____ oh.__

Drill   "Are you a hu-man drone?"
Sergeant: Recruit: "Aye   Sir!"

(I'm gon - na make   you,   I'm gon - na break   you,

I'm gon - na make   you)

a fuck - ing psy - cho,___

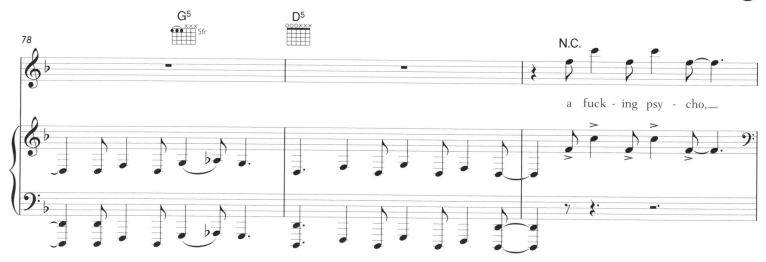

a fuck - ing psy - cho,___

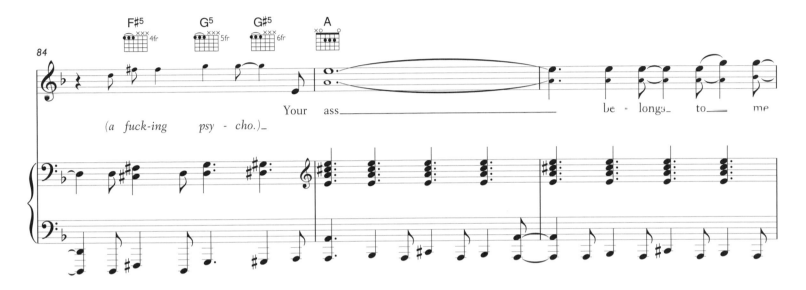

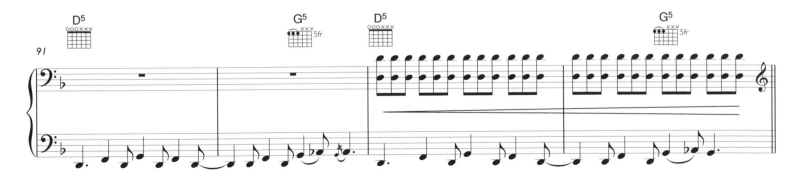

Drill "I will break you,
Sergeant:
do you un-der- stand?

I will break you,
do you un-der- stand?

do you un-der- stand?
I will

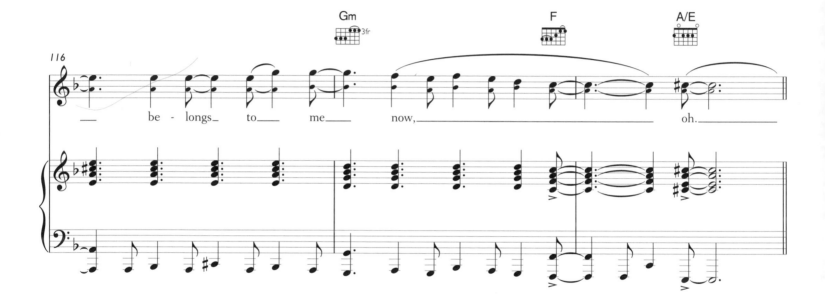

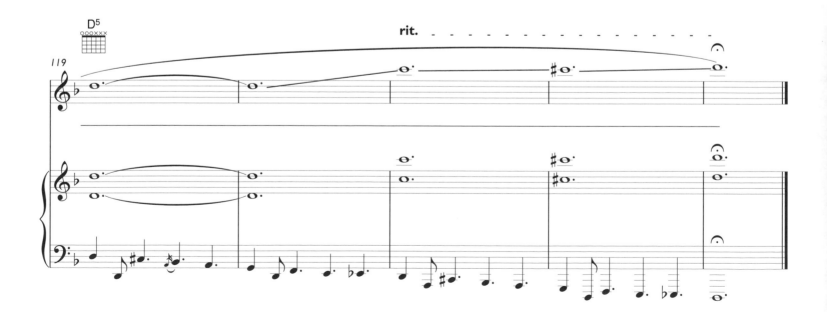

MERCY

WORDS AND MUSIC BY MATTHEW BELLAMY

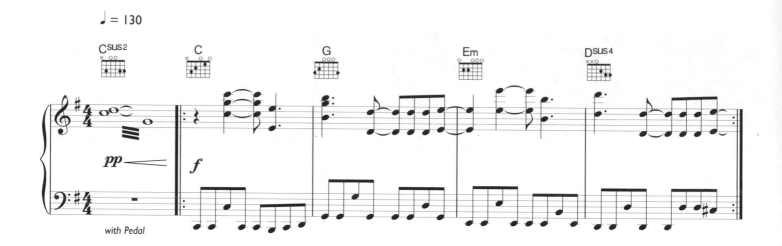

Men— in cloaks,— al - ways seem to, run— the show.— Save— me from the
men— in cloaks, al - ways had to bring— me down.— Run - ning from the

ghosts— and sha - dows— be-fore they eat— my soul,— yeah.
ghosts— and sha - dows, the world just dis - a - vows,— yeah.

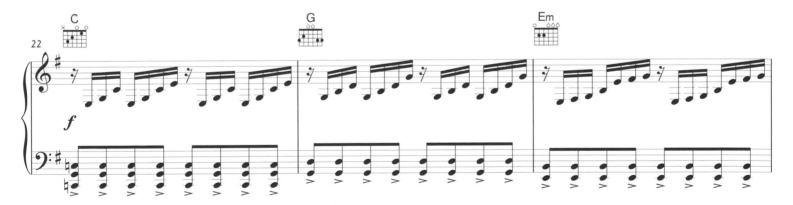

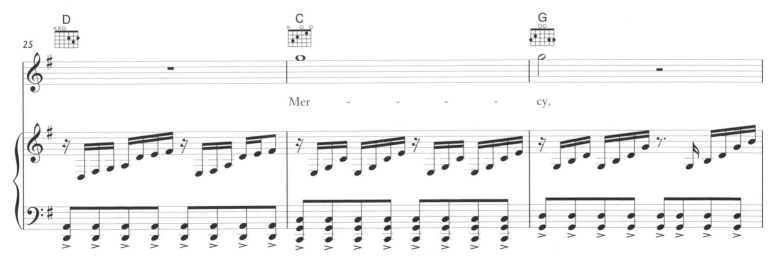

Mer - - - cy,

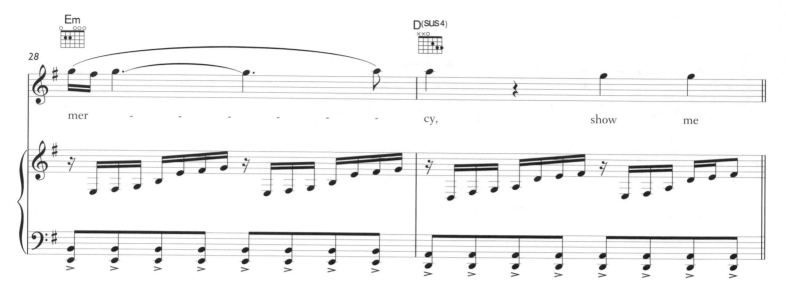

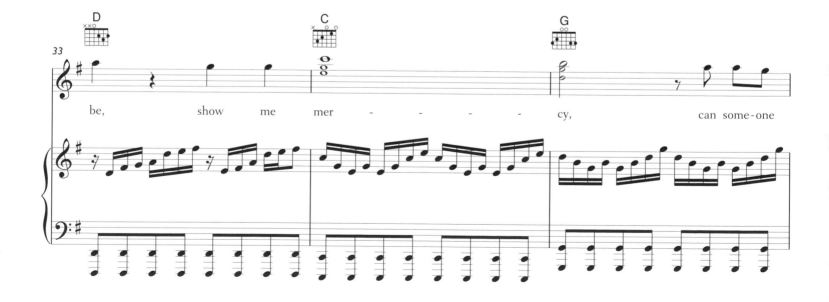

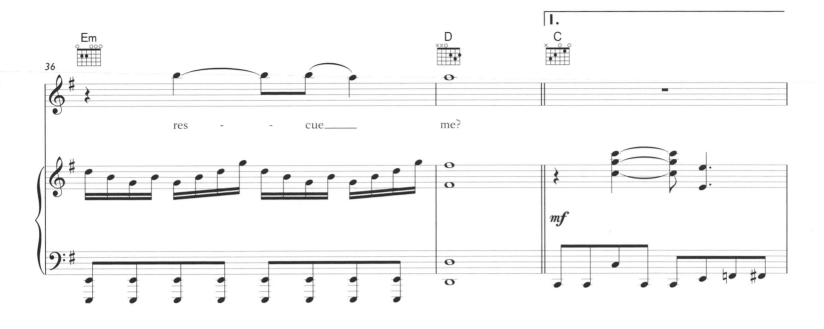

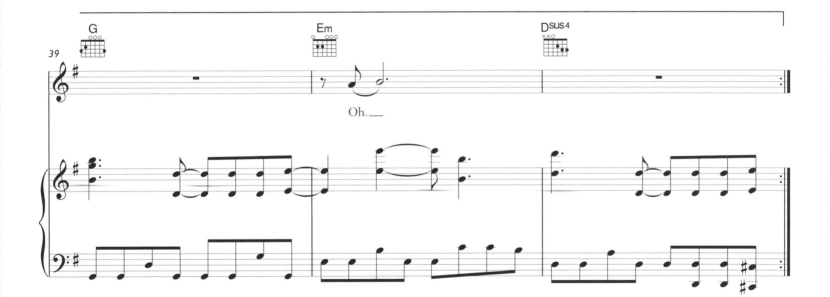

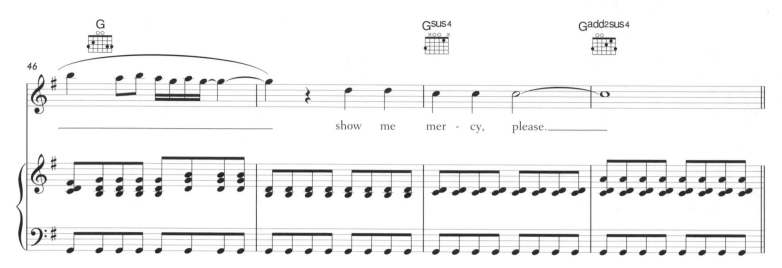

show me mer - cy, please.___

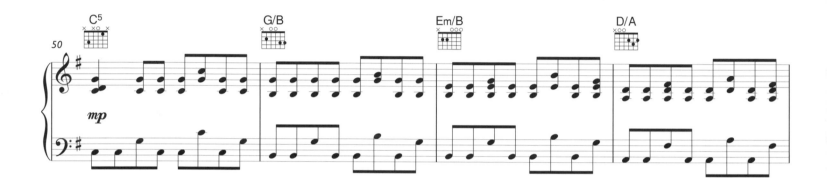

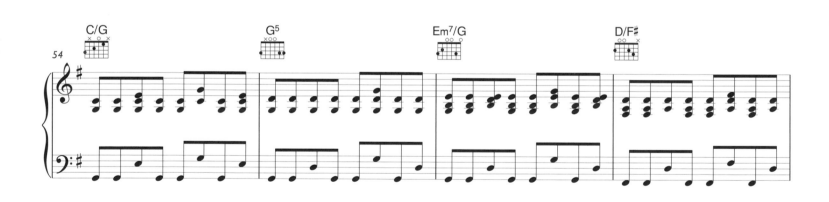

Help me,___ I've fall - en on___ the___ in - side___ and all the

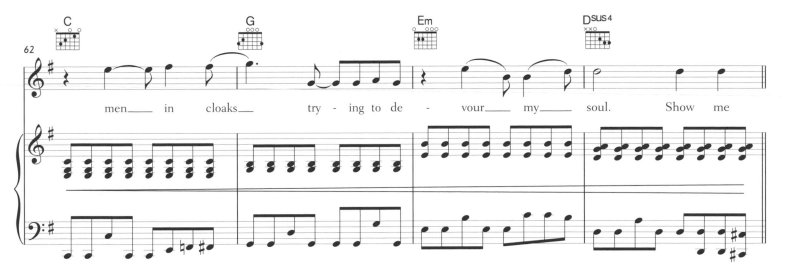

men___ in cloaks___ try - ing to de - vour___ my___ soul. Show me

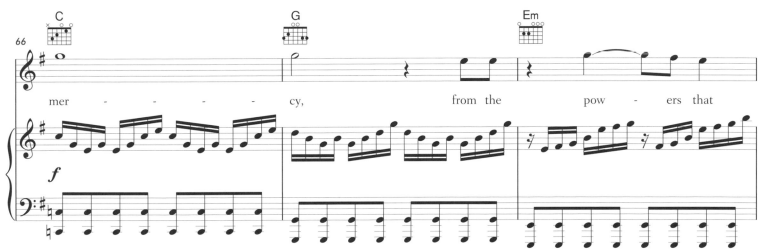

mer - - - cy, from the pow - ers that

be, show me mer - - - cy, from the

gut - less and mean, show me mer - - -

-cy, from the kill - ing ma - chines, show me

mer - - - - cy, can some-one res - cue

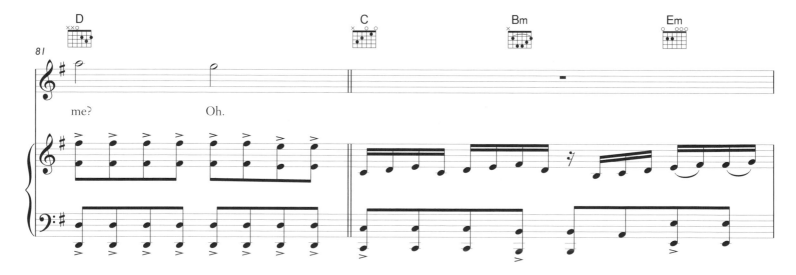

me? Oh.

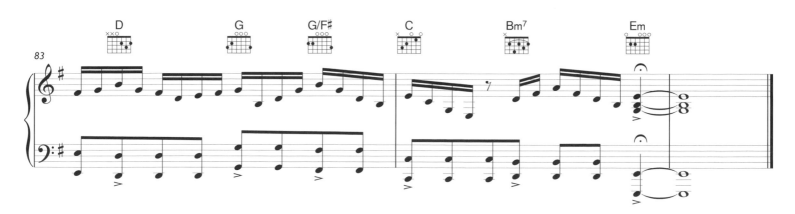

REAPERS

Words and Music by Matthew Bellamy

♩ = 100

Tune Guitar:
6 = D (drop D tuning)

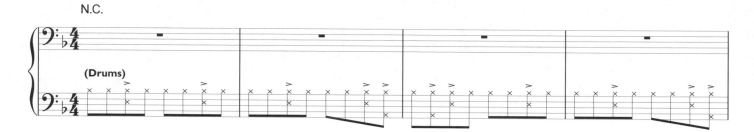

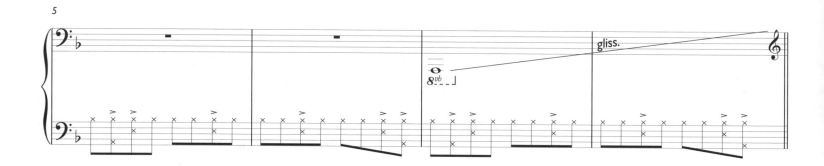

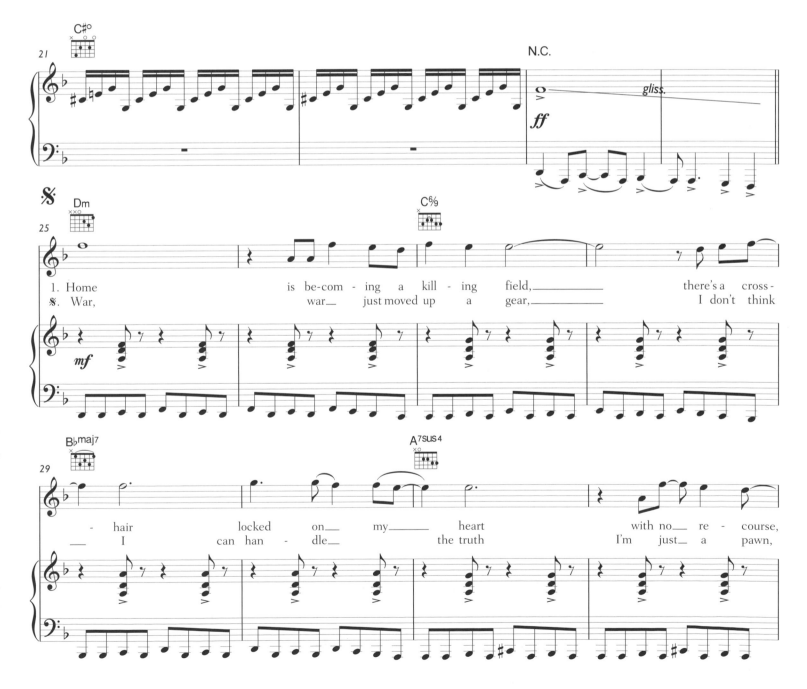

1. Home is be-com - ing a kill - ing field,_____ there's a cross-
War, war_ just moved up a gear,_____ I don't think

-hair locked on_ my_ heart with no re - course,
I can han - dle_ the truth I'm just a pawn,

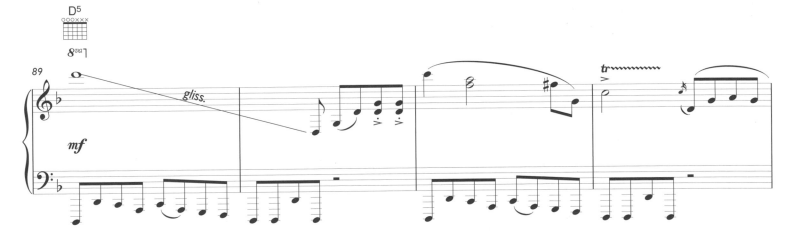

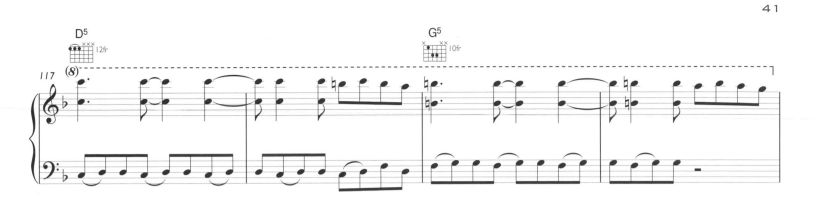

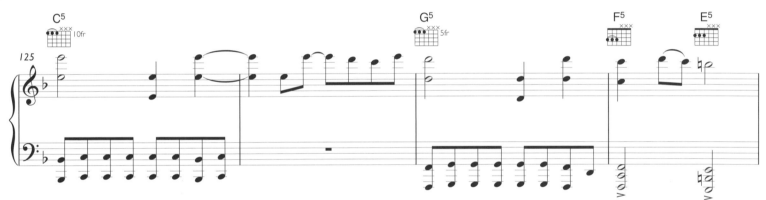

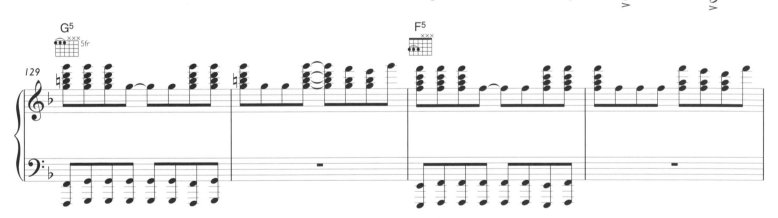

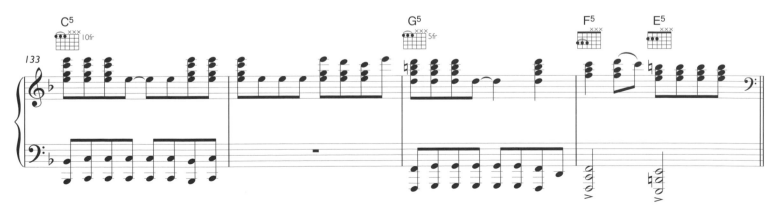

You rule with lies_____ and de-ceit and the
You've got the C. - I. - A.,_____ babe, and

world is_____ on your side._____
all you've done is bru-tal - ise._____

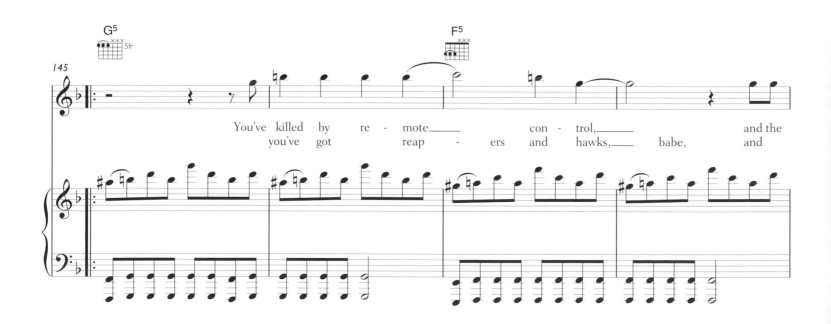

You've killed by re-mote_____ con-trol,_____ and the
you've got reap - ers and hawks,_____ babe, and

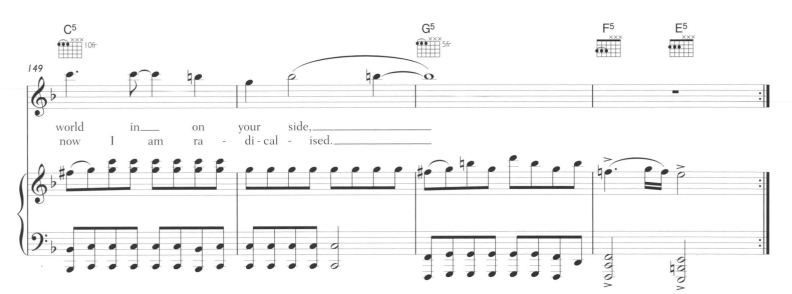

world in___ on your side,_____
now I am ra - di - cal - ised._____

♩ = 120 **Slower**

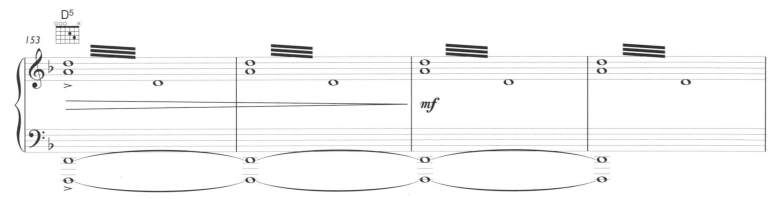

Here come the

Drones.

Here come the

Drones.

rit. _ _ _ _ _ _ _ _ _ _

Free tempo

Noise, FX ad lib.

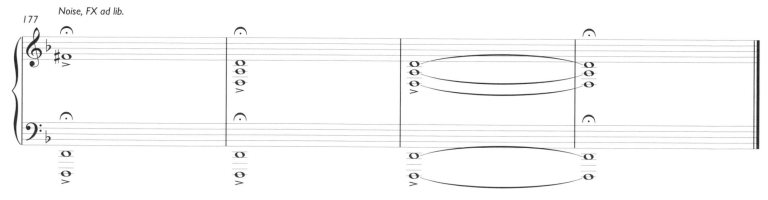

THE HANDLER

Words and Music by Matthew Bellamy

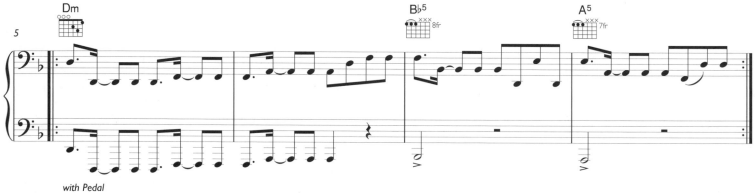

1. You, (you, you) were my_ op-pres - - - sor and_
(2.) -hold, (...hold, ...hold) my trance for-ma - - - tion and_

I, (I, I,) I have_ been prog - rammed to o - bey. And
you, (you, you) are em - pow -ered to do as you please. My

now (now, now) you are my hand - - - - ler and
mind, (mind, mind) was lost in trans - la - - - tion and my

I, (I, I,) I will ex - e - cute your de - mands.
heart, (heart, heart) has be-come a cold and im-pas - sive mach - ine. Leave

me a - lone, I must dis-as-

- so - - ci - - ate from you,

48

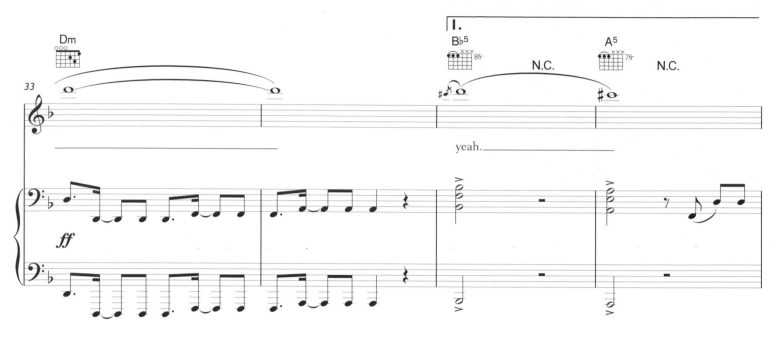

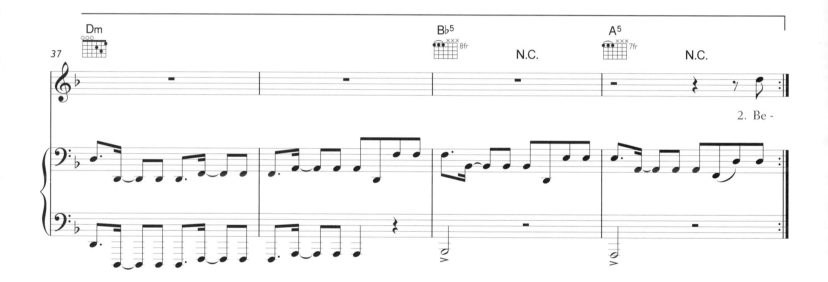

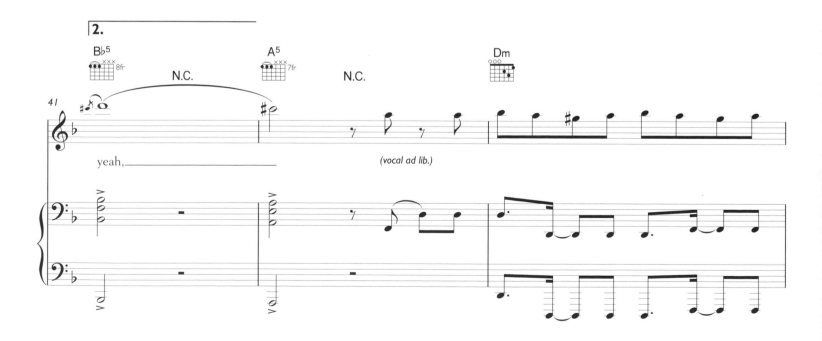

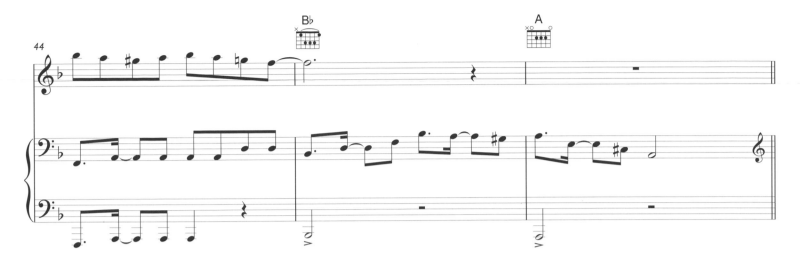

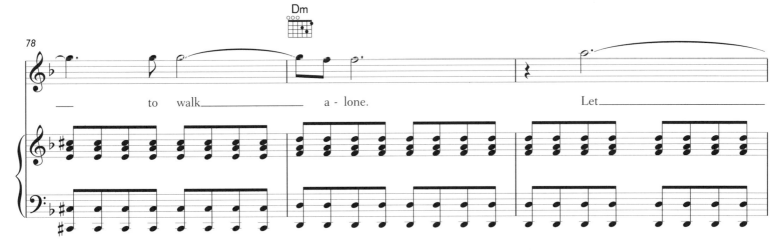

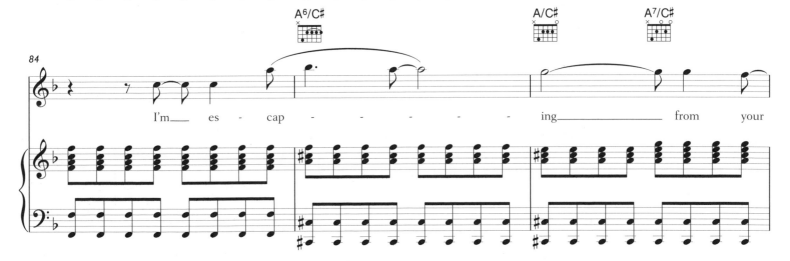

grip._____ You_ will nev-er own me a-gain,

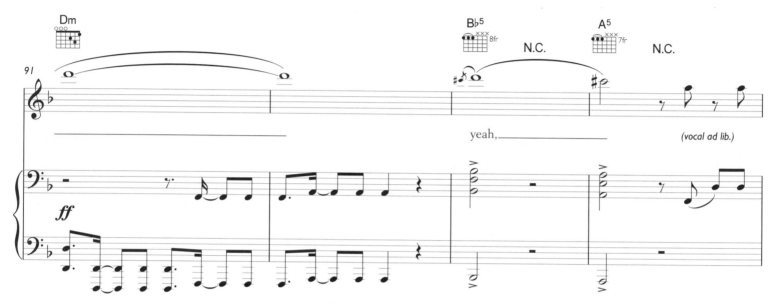

yeah,_____ (vocal ad lib.)

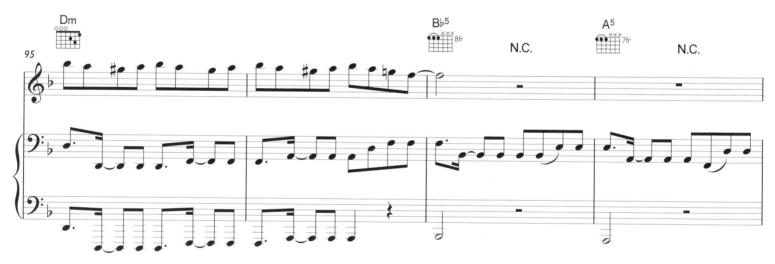

JFK

Music by Matthew Bellamy

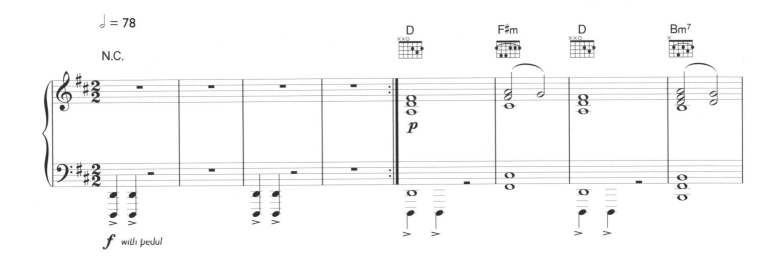

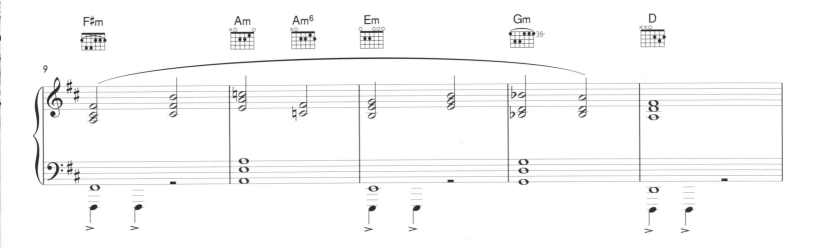

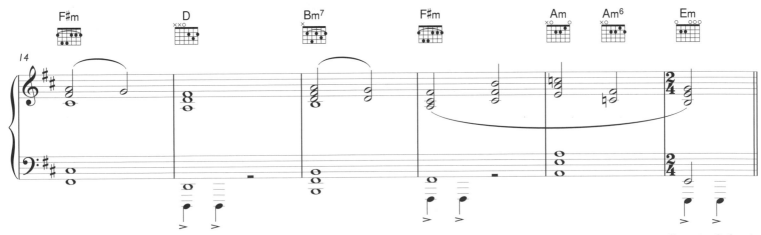

(Segue into Defector)

WE ARE OPPOSED AROUND THE WORLD BY A MONOLITHIC AND RUTHLESS CONSPIRACY THAT RELIES PRIMARILY ON COVERT MEANS FOR EXPANDING ITS SPHERE OF INFLUENCE ON INFILTRATION INSTEAD OF INVASION, ON SUBVERSION INSTEAD OF ELECTIONS, ON INTIMIDATION INSTEAD OF FREE CHOICE, ON GUERRILLAS BY NIGHT INSTEAD OF ARMIES BY DAY. IT IS A SYSTEM WHICH HAS CONSCRIPTED VAST HUMAN AND MATERIAL RESOURCES INTO THE BUILDING OF A TIGHTLY-KNIT,

HIGHLY EFFICIENT MACHINE THAT COMBINES MILITARY, DIPLOMATIC, INTELLIGENCE, ECONOMIC, SCIENTIFIC AND POLITICAL OPERATIONS. ITS PREPARATIONS ARE CONCEALED, NOT PUBLISHED. ITS MISTAKES ARE BURIED, NOT HEADLINED. ITS DISSENTERS ARE SILENCED NOT PRAISED. WE LOOK FOR STRENGTH AND ASSISTANCE, CONFIDENT THAT WITH YOUR HELP, MAN WILL BE WHAT HE WAS BORN TO BE; FREE AND INDEPENDENT.

DEFECTOR

Words and Music by Matthew Bellamy

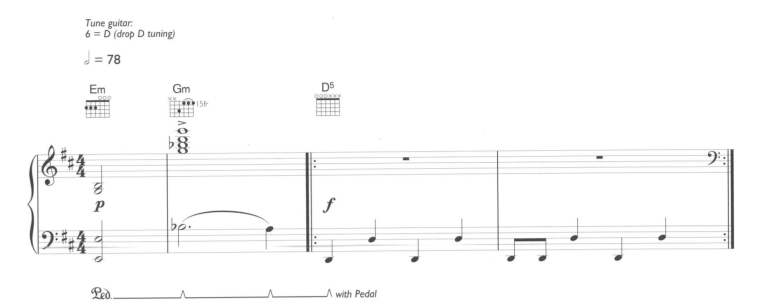

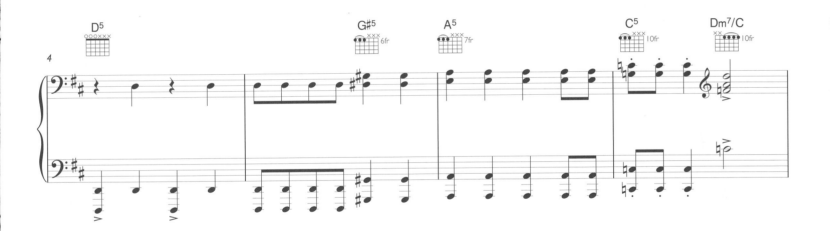

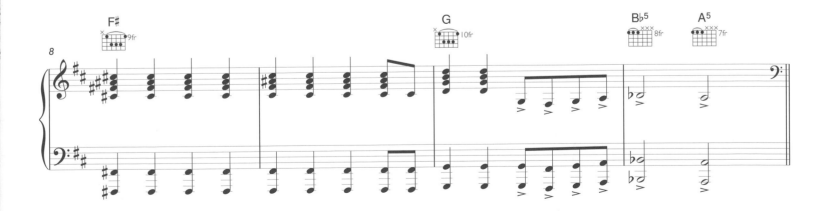

Free,   yeah, I'm____ free   from your___ in-c-c-cit-

-ing,   you can't__ brain-wash me   you've got a prob-lem.___

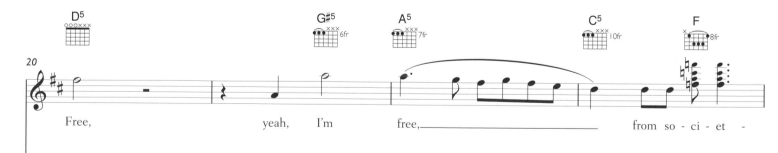

Free,   yeah, I'm   free,_____ from so-ci-et-

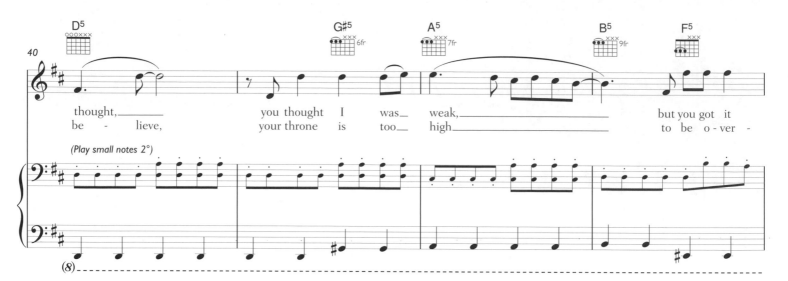

thought,_____ you thought I was__ weak,_____ but you got it
be - lieve, your throne is too__ high_____ to be o - ver -

(Play small notes 2°)

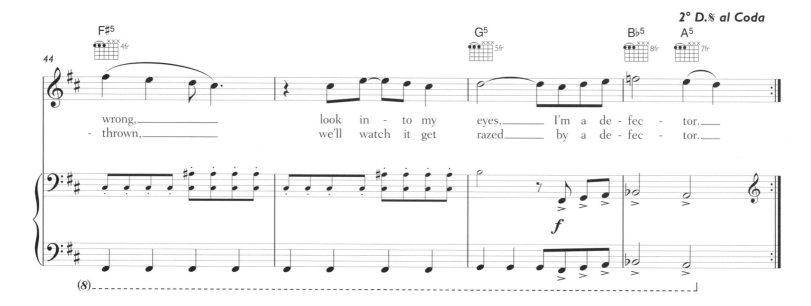

2° D.%. al Coda

wrong,_____ look in - to my eyes,_____ I'm a de - fec - tor.__
- thrown,_____ we'll watch it get razed_____ by a de - fec - tor.__

⊕ Coda

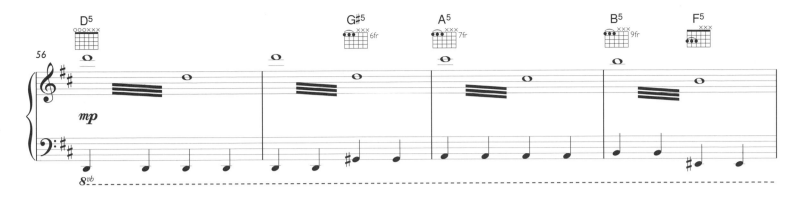

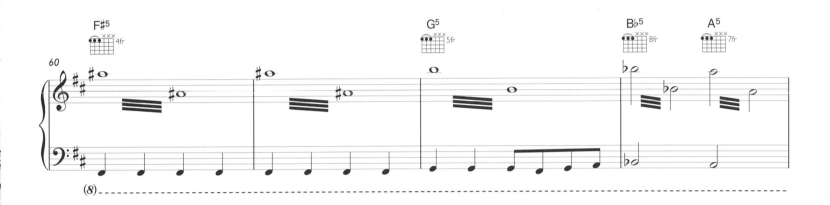

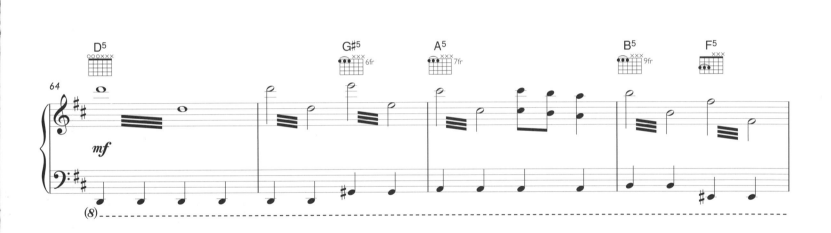

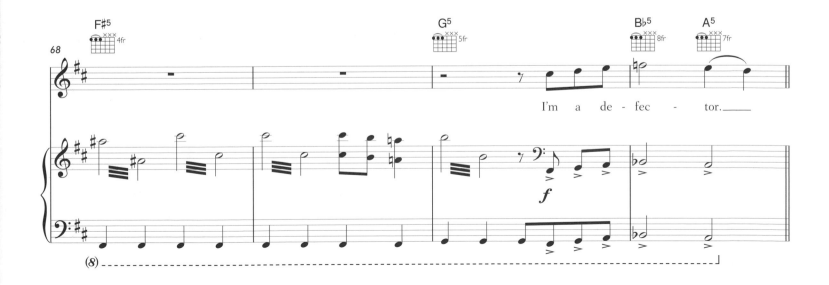

I'm a de - fec - tor.

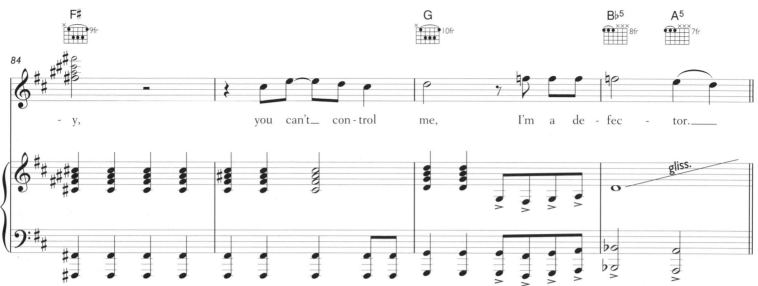

-y, you can't con-trol me, I'm a de - fec - tor. ____

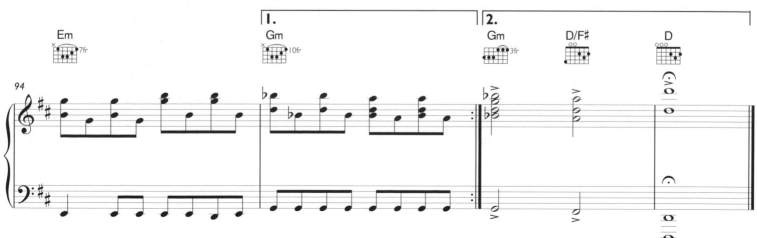

REVOLT

Words and Music by Matthew Bellamy

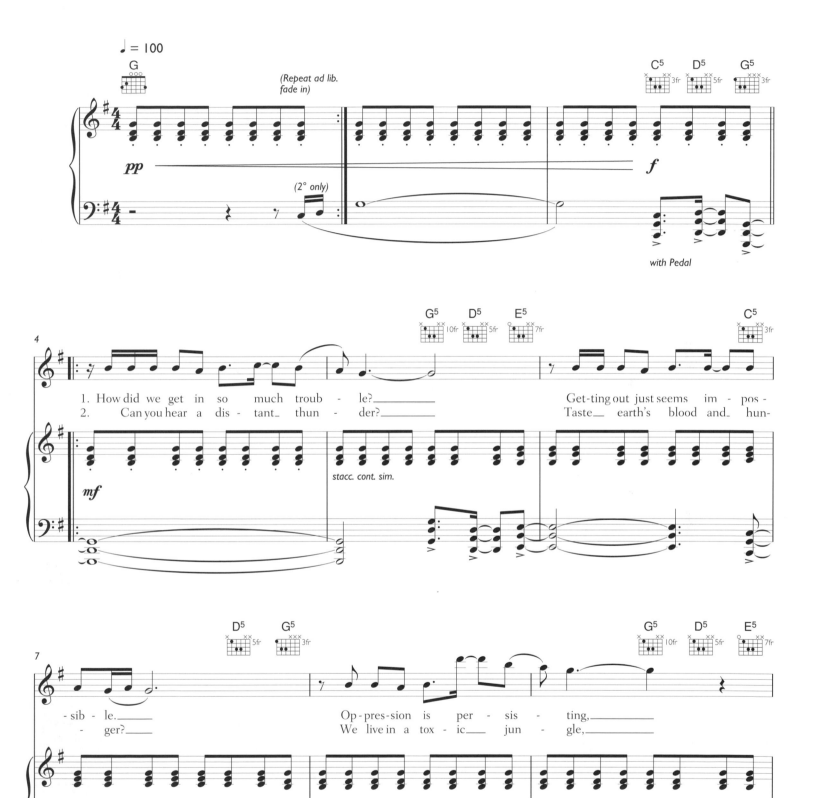

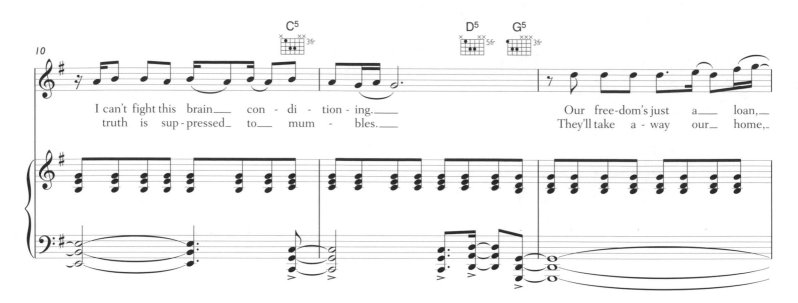

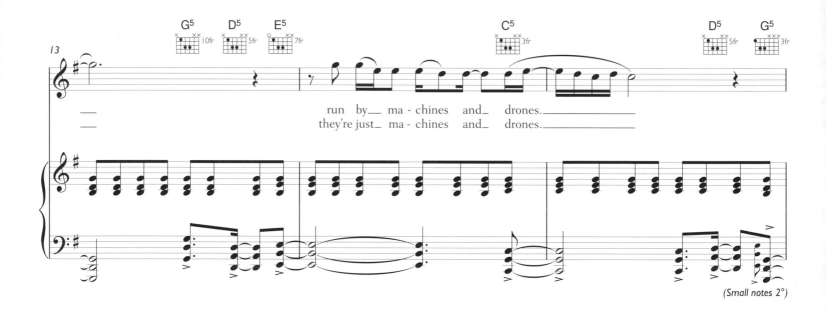

(Small notes 2°)

Omit 2°

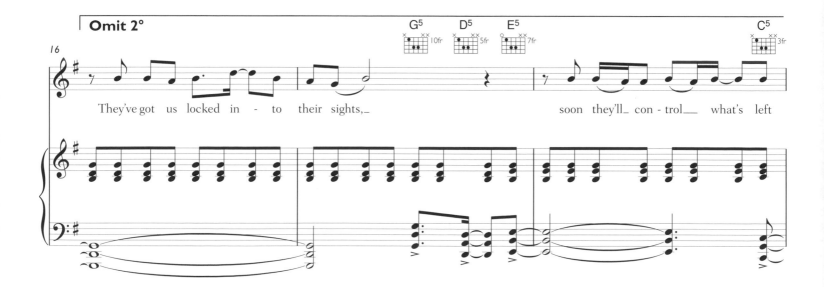

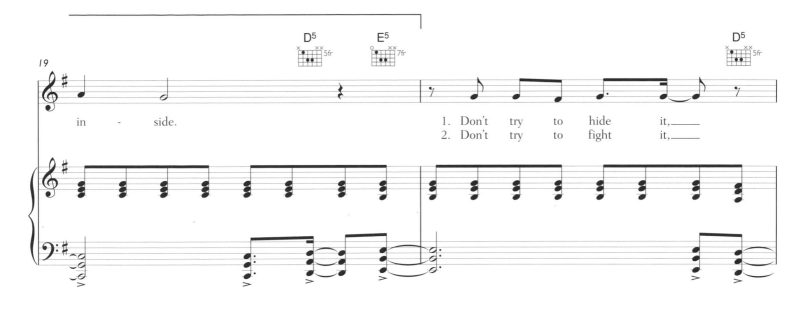

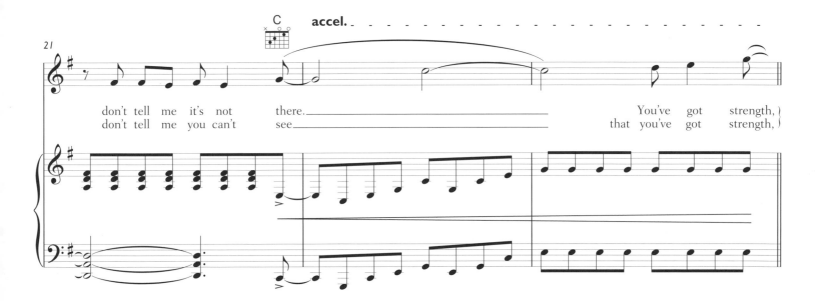

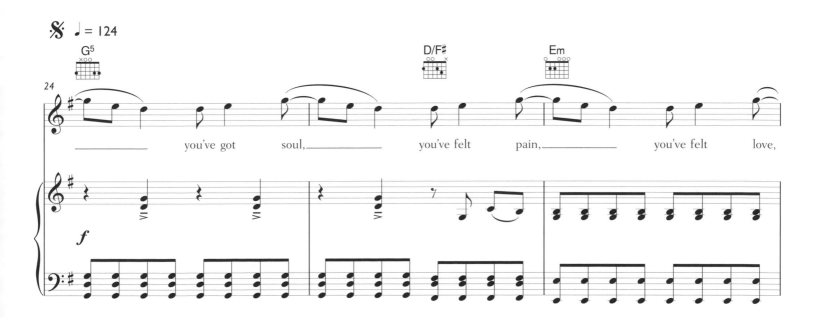

you can grow,_____ you can grow,___ you can make
(You can grow,_ you can grow.)_

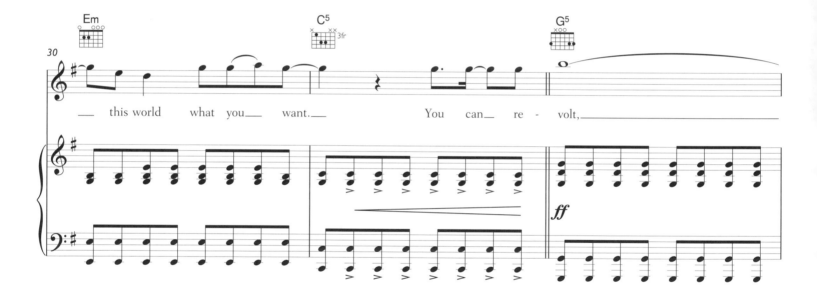

_ this world what you___ want.___ You can__ re - volt,_____

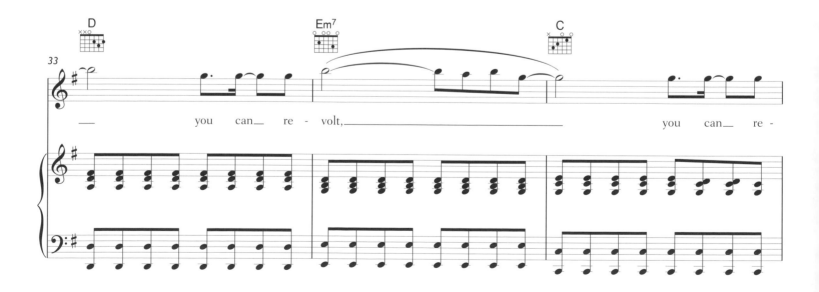

__ you can re - volt,_____ you can re -

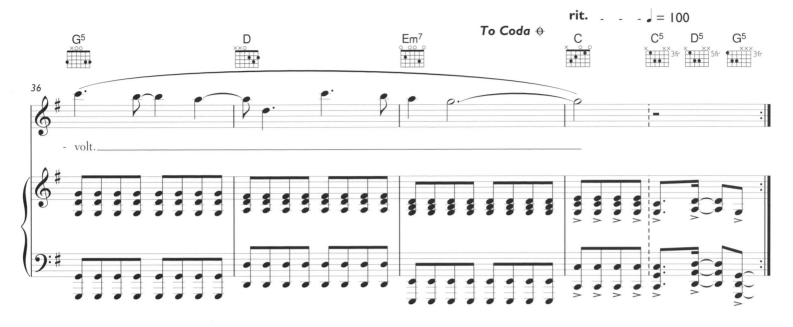

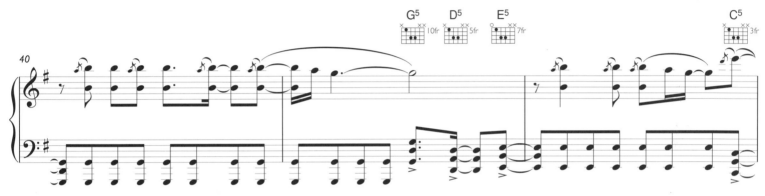

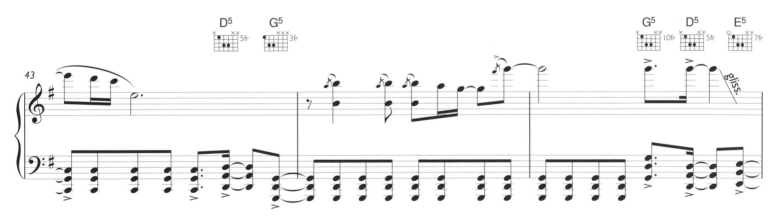

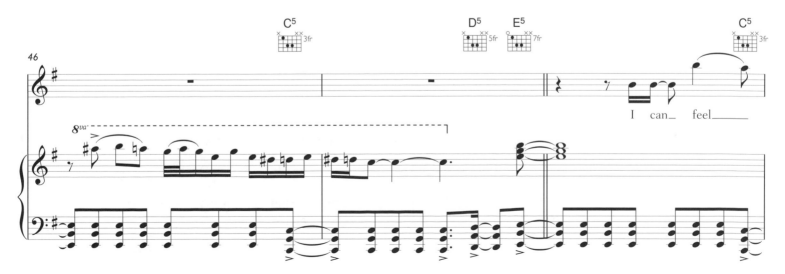

I can feel

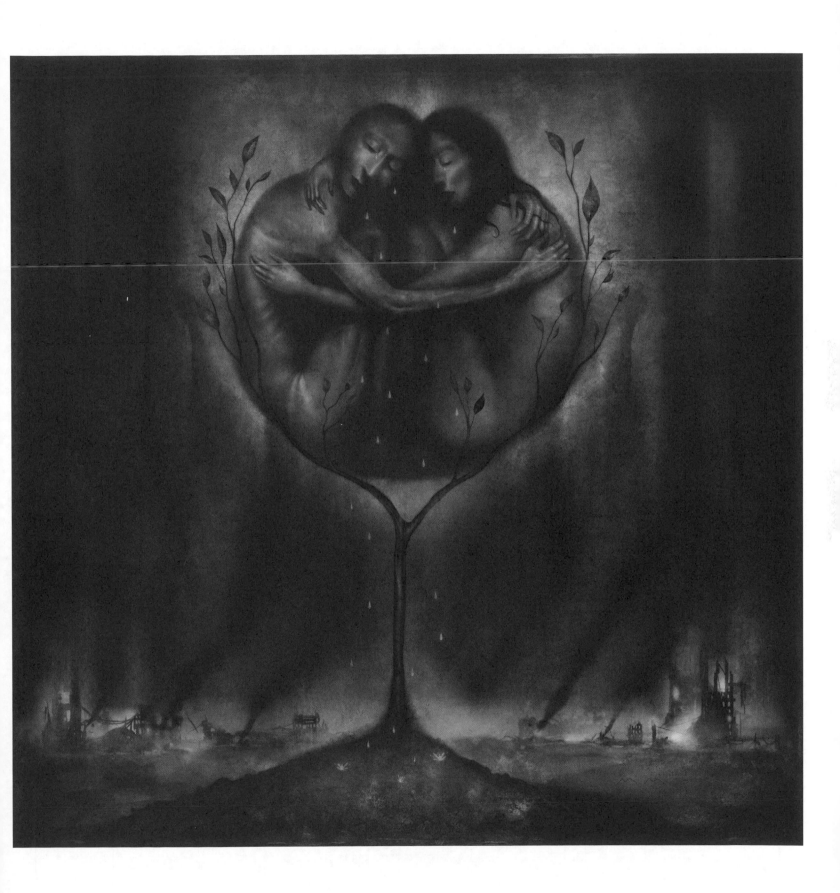

AFTERMATH

Words and Music by Matthew Bellamy

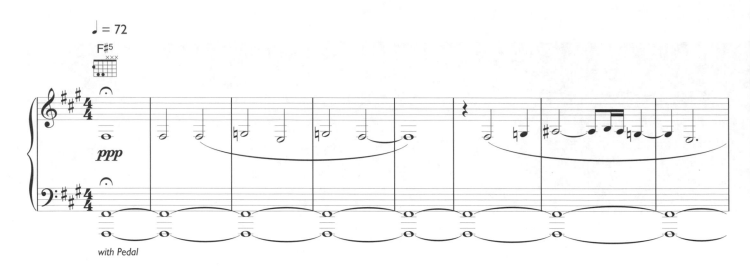

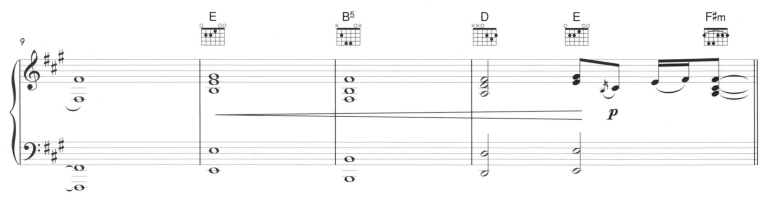

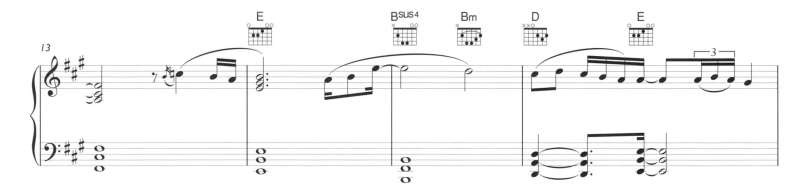

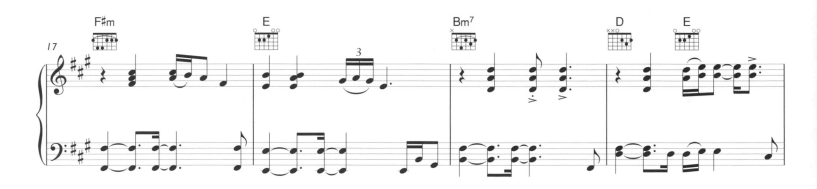

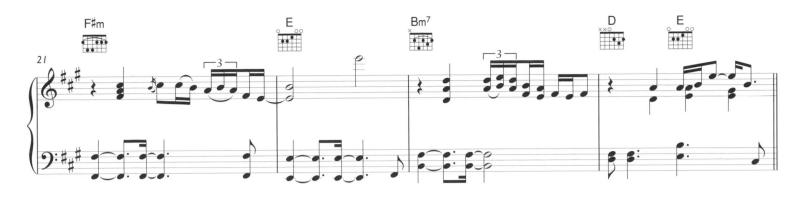

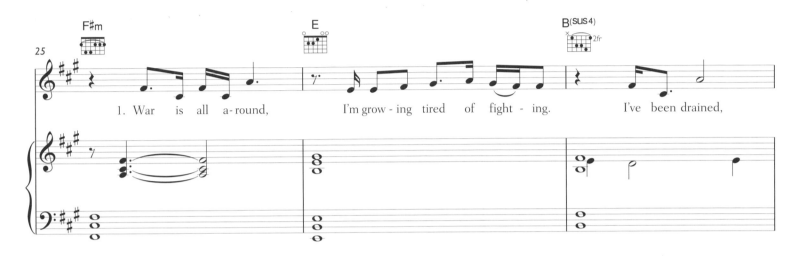

1. War is all a-round, I'm grow-ing tired of fight-ing. I've been drained,

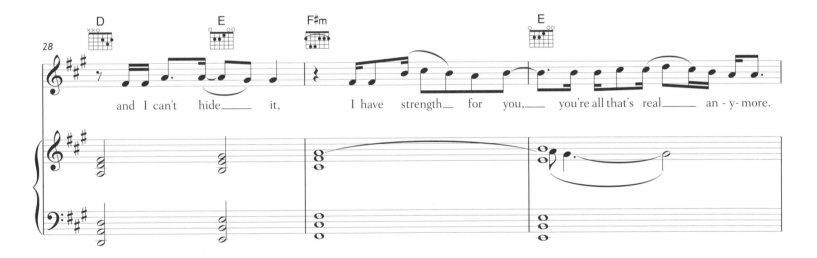

and I can't hide____ it, I have strength____ for you,____ you're all that's real____ an-y-more.

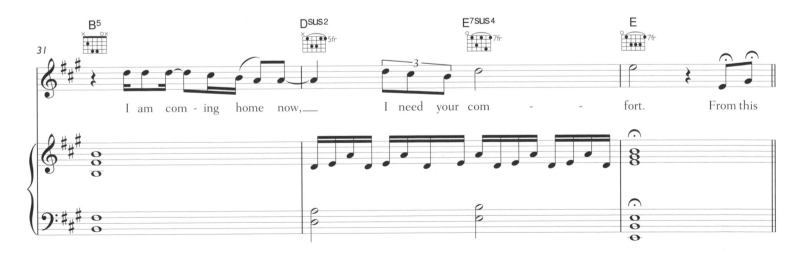

I am com-ing home now,____ I need your com - - fort. From this

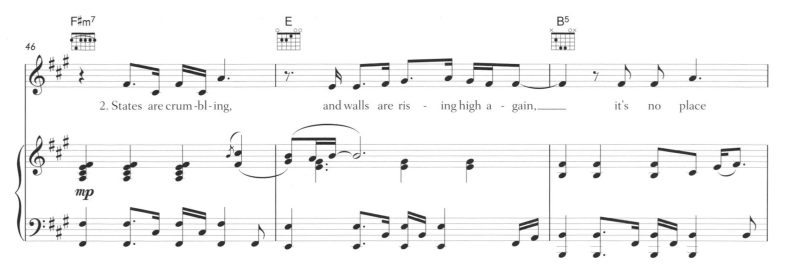

2. States are crum-bl-ing, and walls are ris - ing high a - gain,___ it's no place

for the___ faint - heart - ed. But my heart___ is strong,___ be-cause now I know where I___ be-long.

it's you and I___ a - gainst the world, we are free___ from this mom - ent, from this

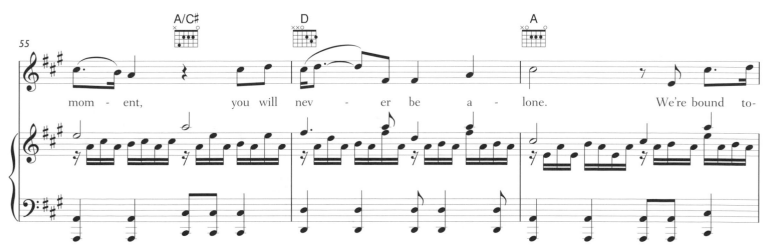

mom - ent, you will nev - er be a - lone. We're bound to-

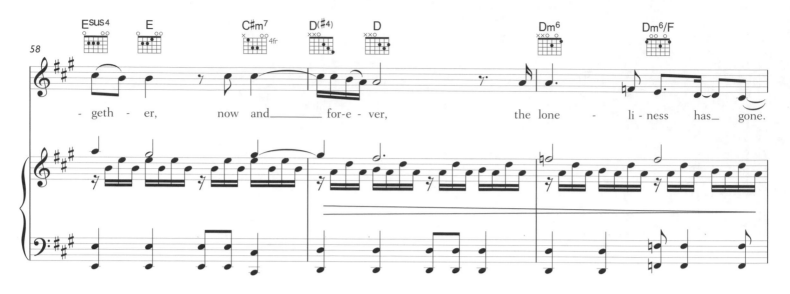

-geth - er, now and_____ for-e - ver, the lone - li - ness has_ gone.

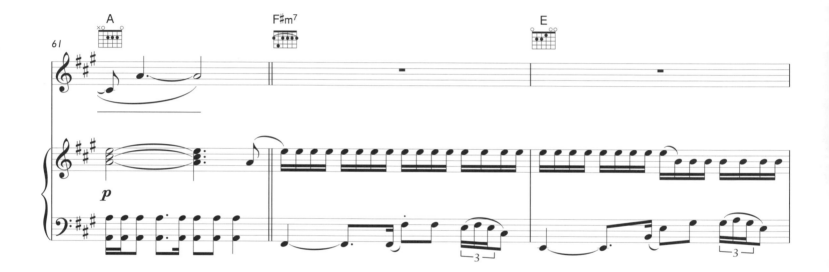

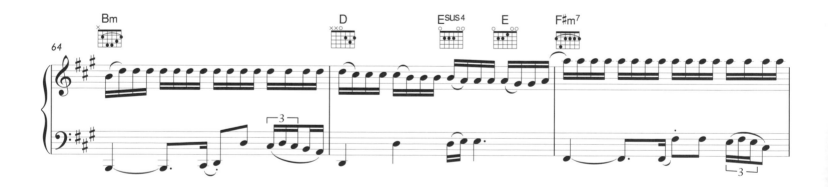

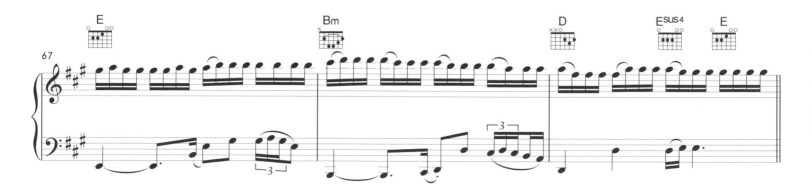

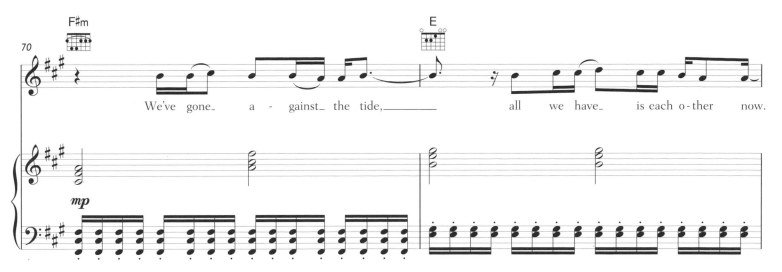

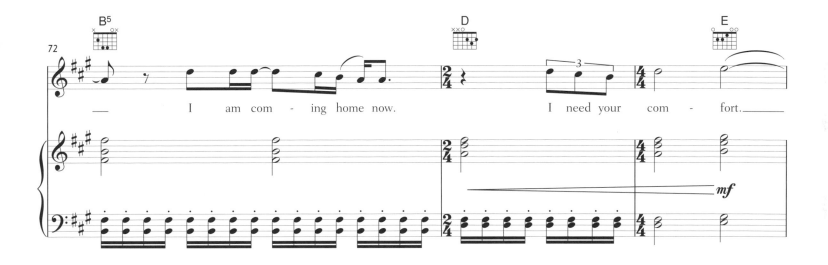

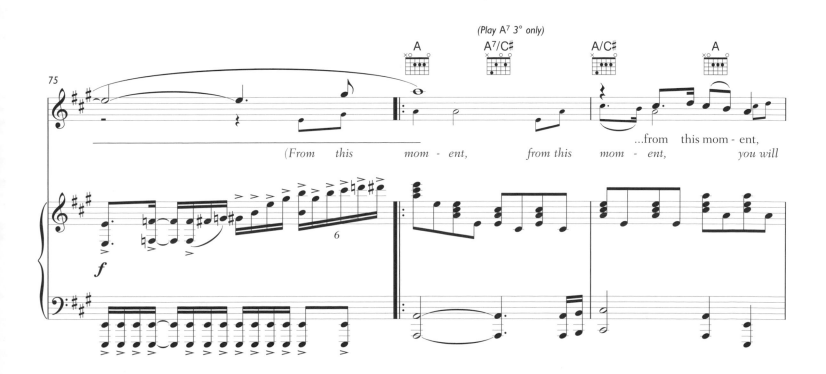

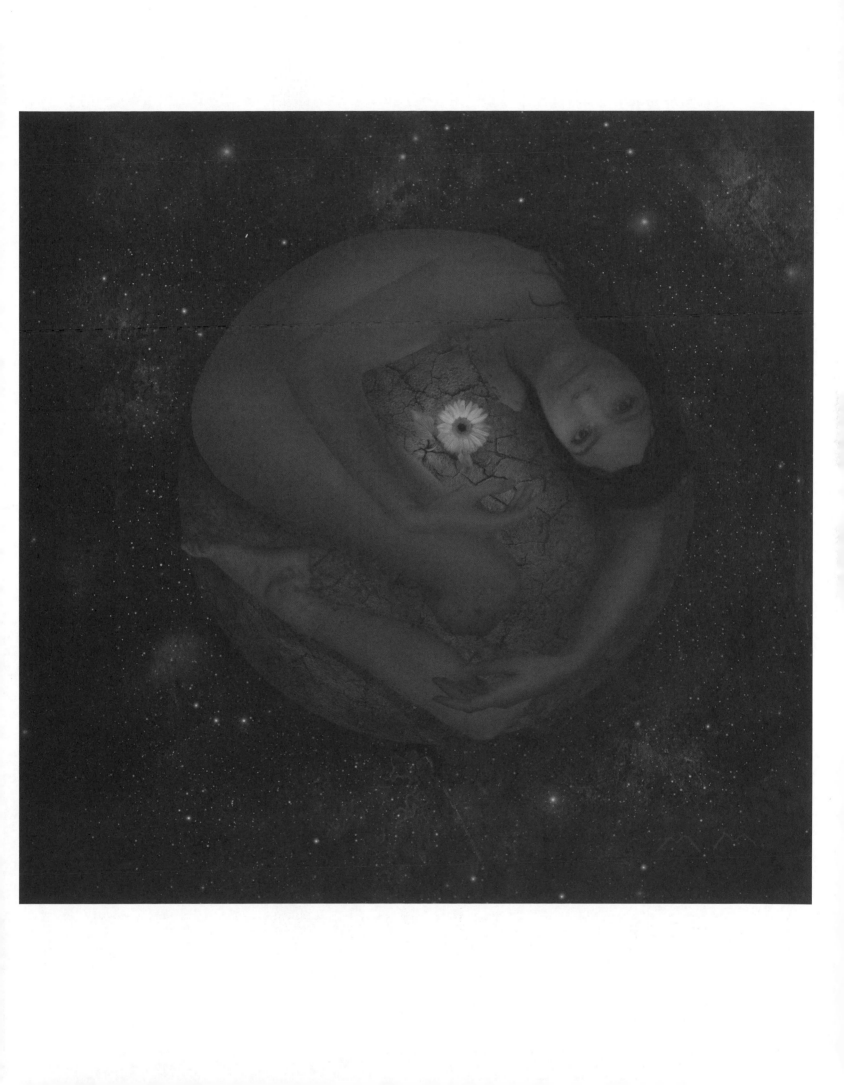

THE GLOBALIST

Words and Music by Matthew Bellamy

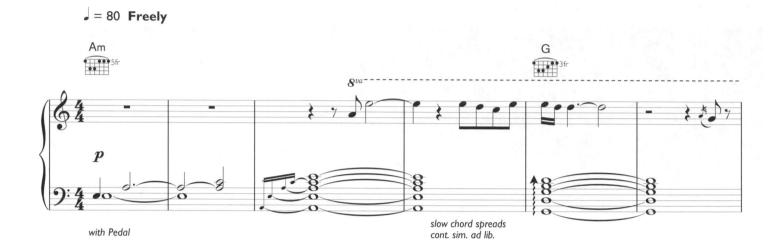

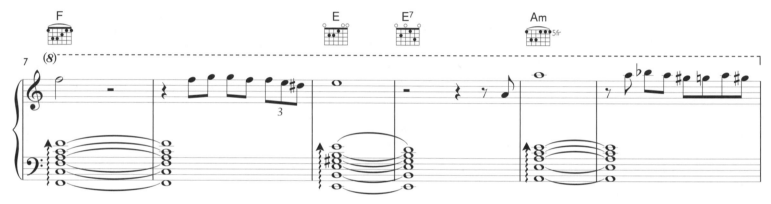

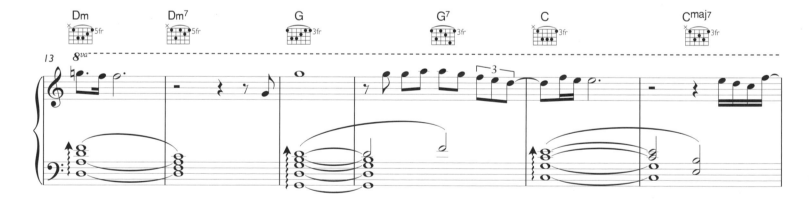

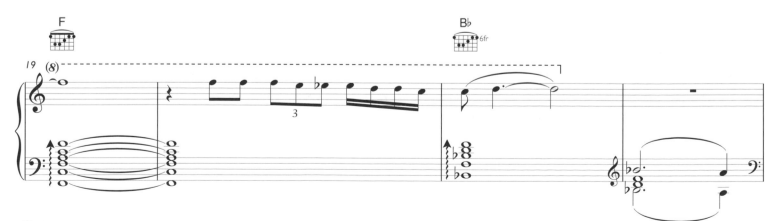

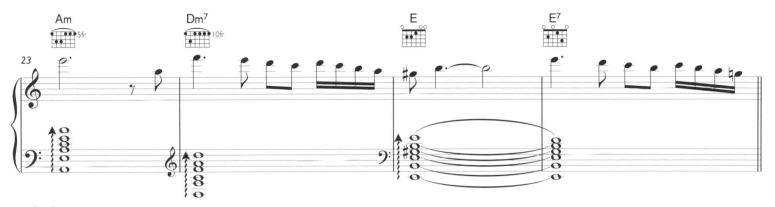

Strict tempo

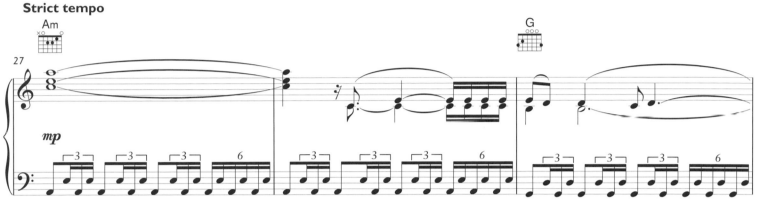

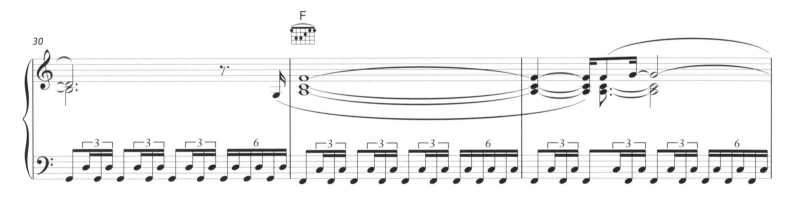

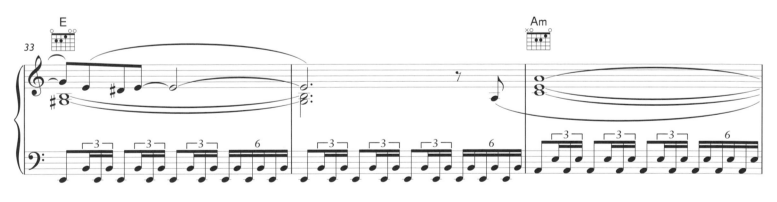

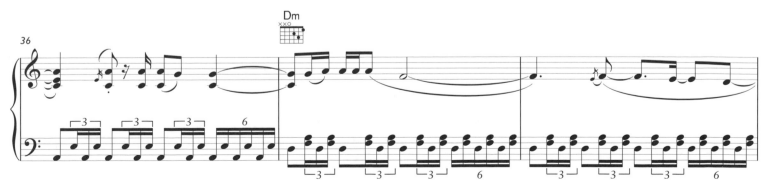

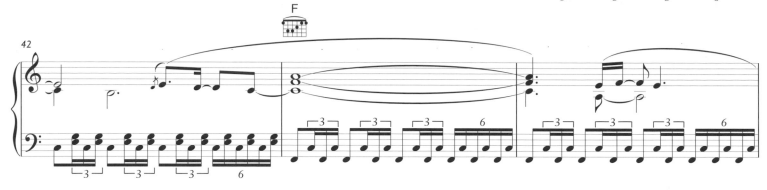

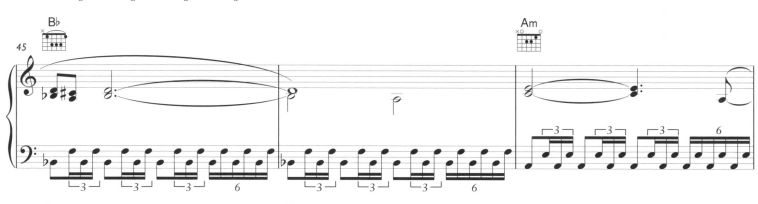

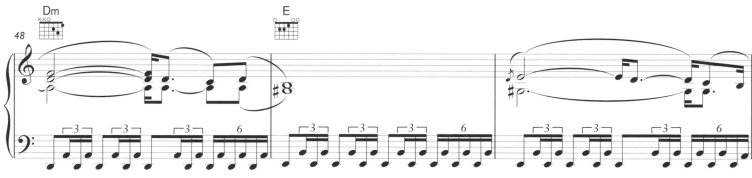

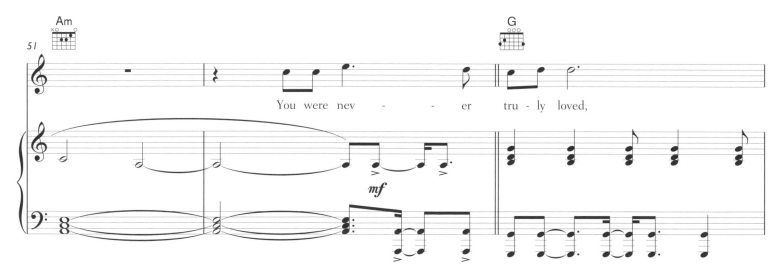

You were nev - - er tru - ly loved,

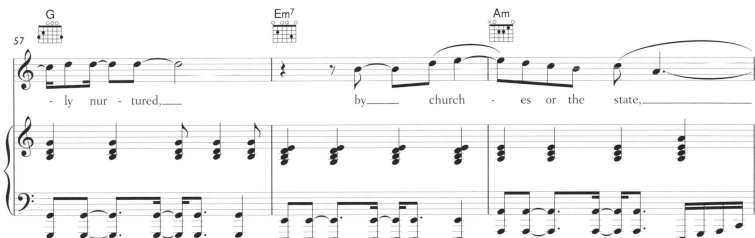

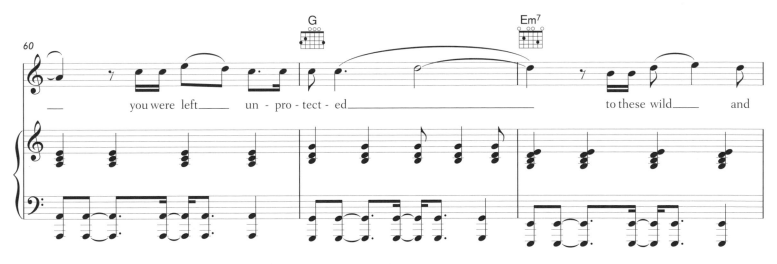

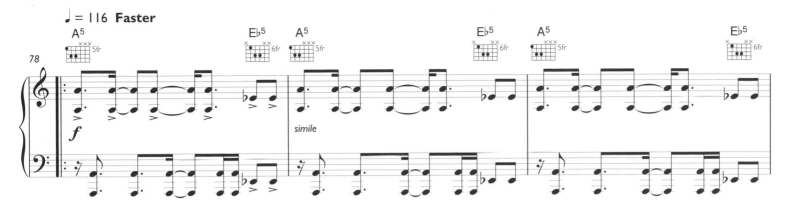

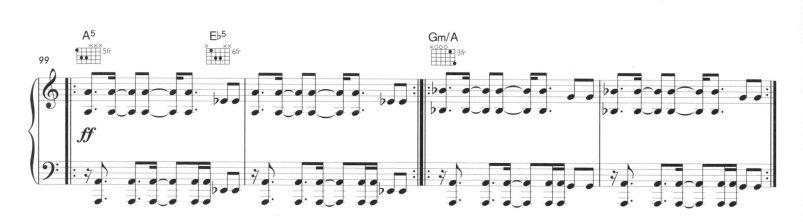

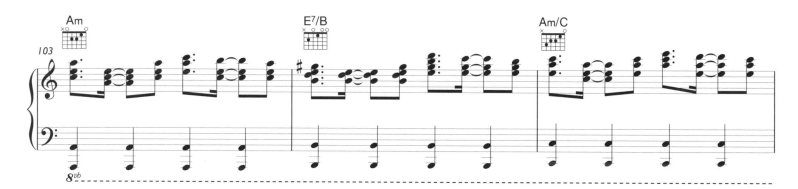

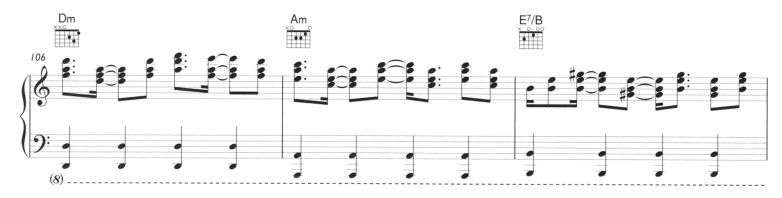

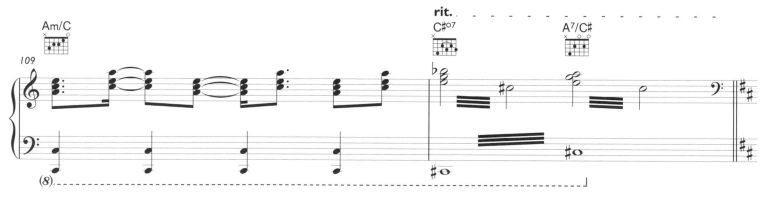

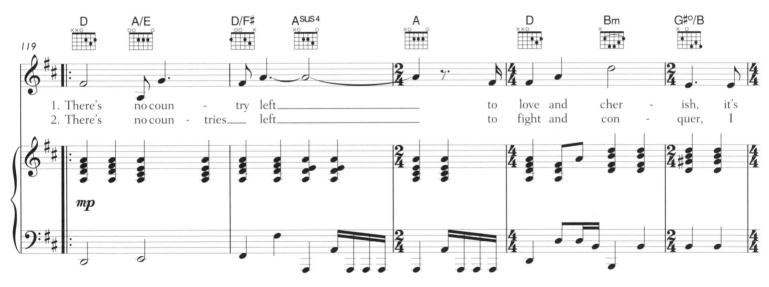

1. There's no coun - try left_____ to love and cher - ish, it's
2. There's no coun - tries__ left_____ to fight and con - quer, I

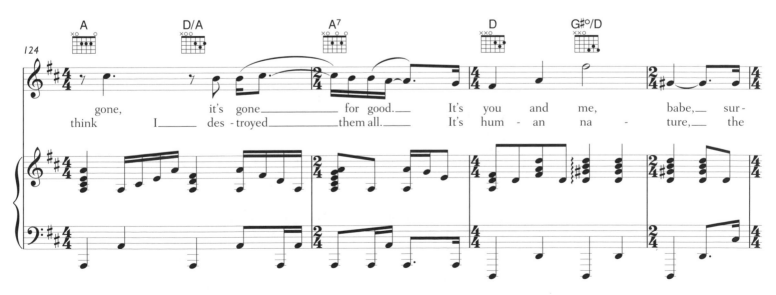

gone, it's gone_____ for good.__ It's you and me, babe,__ sur -
think I__ des - troyed__ them all.__ It's hum - an na - ture,__ the

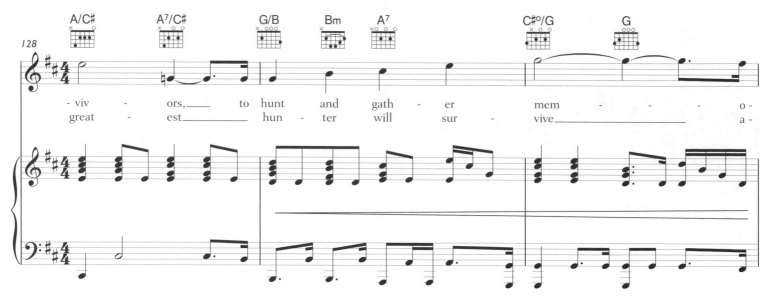

-viv - ors,___ to hunt and gath - er mem - - - o-
great - est___ hun - ter will sur - vive___ a-

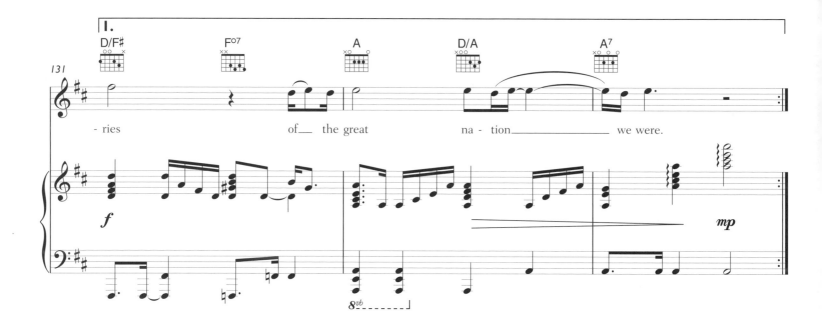

1.

-ries of__ the great na - tion___ we were.

2.

- lone with no - one left to__ love.___

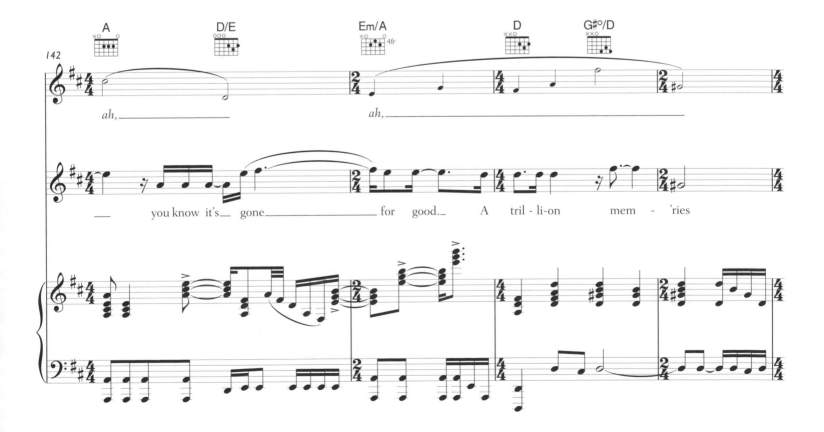

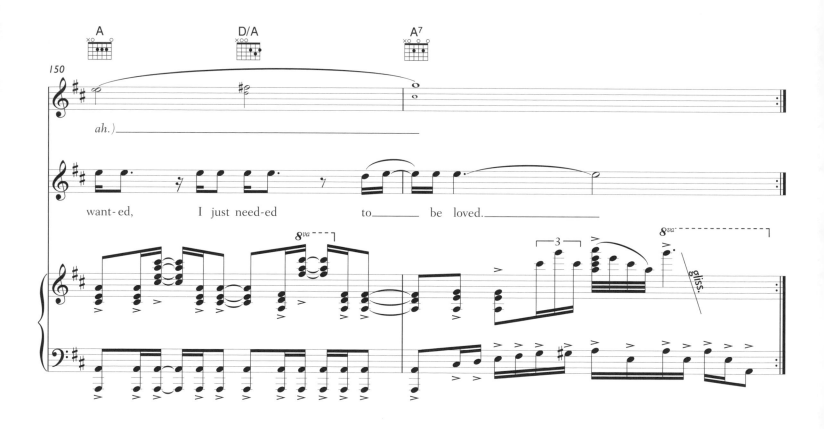

(Segue into Drones)

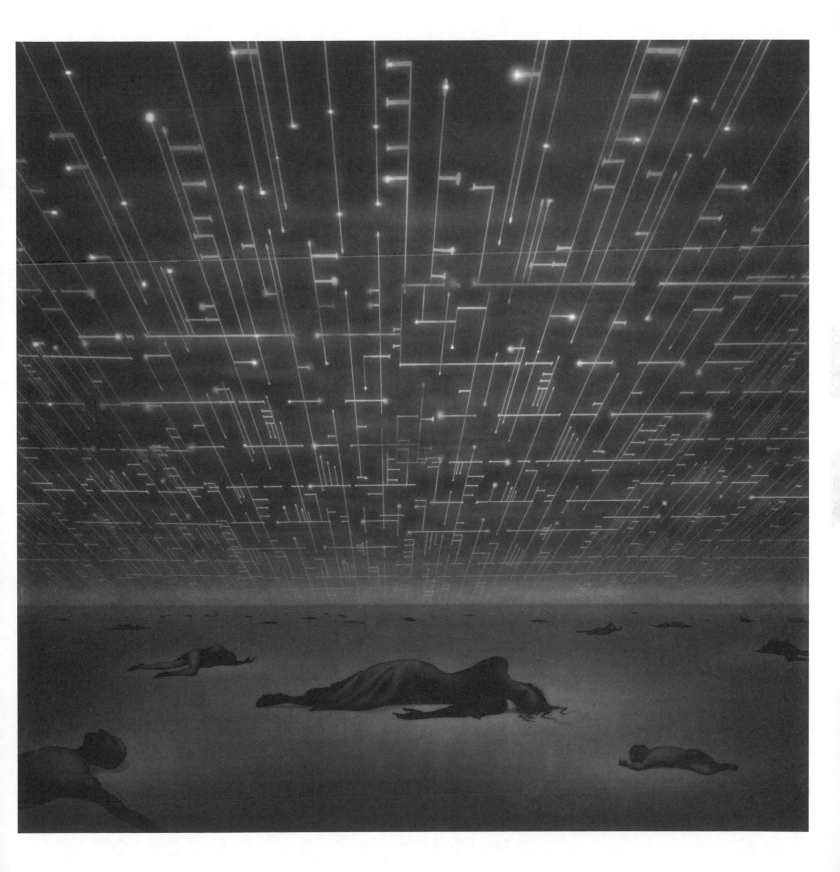

DRONES

Words and Music by Matthew Bellamy

21

Can you___ feel___ an - y- thing?

___ be-tween, can you feel an - y - thing, can you feel an - y - thing?

Can___ you feel an - - - y - thing? Can

Can___ you feel an - y - thing, an - y - thing? Can___

26

Are you___ dead?Are you___ dead___ in - side?___

Are___ you dead___ in - side?

you___ feel__ an - y - thing? Are you dead in-

___ you? Are you___ dead in - side? Are you___ dead in -

Now you_____ can kill____ from the_____
Now you____ can_____ kill,_____ the
- side?_____ From the___ safe - ty of your home,
- side?_____ Now you can kill_____ from the safe - ty,

safe - ty your home with Drones. A - - - a - men.
safe - ty of your home with Drones. A - - - - men.
of your_____ home,___ your_ home with Drones. A - - - - men.
from the safe - ty of your home with Drones. A - - - - men.